A HISTORY
OF
Fashion

ESSENTIAL LIBRARY OF CULTURAL HISTORY

A HISTORY OF *Fashion*

by Rebecca Rissman

Content Consultant
Jeffrey C. Mayer
Associate Professor of Fashion Design
Curator, Sue Ann Genet Costume Collection and Research Center
Syracuse University

An Imprint of Abdo Publishing | www.abdopublishing.com

www.abdopublishing.com

Published by Abdo Publishing, a division of ABDO, PO Box 398166, Minneapolis, Minnesota 55439. Copyright © 2015 by Abdo Consulting Group, Inc. International copyrights reserved in all countries. No part of this book may be reproduced in any form without written permission from the publisher. Essential Library™ is a trademark and logo of Abdo Publishing.

Printed in the United States of America, North Mankato, Minnesota
102014
012015

Cover Photo: iStockphoto
Interior Photos: Georgios Kollidas/Shutterstock Images, 1 (left), 45; R. Gino Santa Maria/ Shutterstock Images, 1 (right), 86; Harry Hu/Shutterstock Images, 3 (top), 89; Everett Collection/Shutterstock Images, 3 (bottom), 70; Heritage Images/Corbis, 7; AP Images, 11, 101; Shutterstock Images, 13, 16, 19, 26, 37 (top), 37 (bottom), 42, 98; Elliotte Rusty Harold/Shutterstock Images, 23; Hein Nouwens/Shutterstock Images, 29, 39; Corbis, 31; Gianni Dagli Orti/Corbis, 32; Photos.com/Thinkstock, 35; Leemage/Corbis, 49; The Gallery Collection/Corbis, 52; Public Domain, 54, 62, 100; Stapleton Collection/Corbis, 57; Library of Congress, 60, 64, 99; Hodag Media/Shutterstock Images, 67; Everett Collection/ Glow Images, 71 (top), 71 (bottom); Underwood & Underwood/Corbis, 73; Bettmann/ Corbis, 79; GraphicaArtis/Corbis, 81; Hulton-Deutch Collection/Corbis, 84; Phil Noble/ EMPPL PA Wire/AP Images, 90; Leonhard Foeger/Reuters/Corbis, 96

Editor: Jennifer Anderson
Series Designer: Maggie Villaume

Library of Congress Control Number: 2014943873

Cataloging-in-Publication Data

Rissman, Rebecca.
 A history of fashion / Rebecca Rissman.
  p. cm. -- (Essential library of cultural history)
ISBN 978-1-62403-553-1 (lib. bdg.)
Includes bibliographical references and index.
1. Fashion--History--Juvenile literature.   I. Title.
391.009--dc23

                                                                2014943873

CONTENTS

Chapter 1

The Colorful History of Fashion

*F*rom towering wigs to plunging necklines, cinched corsets to padded shoulders, fashion has always been a colorful reflection of culture. The word *fashion* can refer to any popular trend, but it most often refers to the clothing, footwear, makeup, hairstyles, jewelry, and other accessories that are in style at a particular time and place.

Early fashion was simple and functional, designed for protection from the elements. Crude sandals shielded people's feet from the rough ground. Furs and animal skins were used for warmth more than for beauty. But archaeological evidence shows that even prehistoric

Napoléon Bonaparte's clothing at his coronation in 1804 advertised the power of the new French Empire.

The oldest shoes
ever found date
back to 8,500 BCE.
Archaeologists
discovered the
10,500-year-old
sandals, woven
from tree bark, in a
cave in Oregon.[2]

people liked to decorate themselves with shells, bones, and other natural materials.

As people learned to sew and weave, fashion became more sophisticated. Different cuts and colors of clothing could indicate a person's gender, religion, occupation, and social rank. Fashion became, as it is today, an important part of culture as well as a complex and often beautiful art form.

Major Moments in Fashion History

Some of the world's notable historical events show that fashion can make a powerful political statement. When Napoléon Bonaparte was crowned emperor of France in 1804, he wore clothes designed to awe and impress. Napoléon wore long satin robes under a red velvet cape that was embroidered with golden bees and lined in ermine fur. The cape weighed more than 80 pounds (36 kg) and required four men to carry it.[1] Napoléon's wife, Empress Josephine, also wore a luxurious red velvet cape over an exquisite white silk gown, as well as a diamond and pearl crown. The elaborate and magnificent styles sent a message to the world: the French Republic was now the grand and mighty French Empire. Over the next decade, France would become the dominant power in Western Europe.

In the summer of 1968, racial tension in the United States was high. Martin Luther King Jr. had just been assassinated, and riots were breaking out in US cities. At the Olympic Games that summer, African-American athletes Tommie Smith and John Carlos used fashion as a form of social protest. As they stood on the awards podium to accept their medals, each wore one black glove. When the American anthem began to play, they raised their gloved fists in a salute representing

Three Billion People Watching One Dress

Royal fashions have always fascinated the public. This was obvious in 1981 when Lady Diana Spencer married Prince Charles, heir to the throne of the United Kingdom. Diana's romantic, full-skirted ivory satin gown with puffed sleeves and a 25-foot (8 m) train made her a fashion sensation. In 2011, the wedding of Kate Middleton to Prince William, Charles and Diana's son, drew an estimated 3 billion viewers.[3] Middleton's choice of a wedding dress was kept secret until just before the ceremony. When she stepped out of the royal car to enter Westminster Abbey, the waiting crowd gasped and cheered. Middleton's dress, designed by Sarah Burton of the British fashion house of Alexander McQueen, featured long lace sleeves. Brides around the world began imitating her look.

SOCIAL CHANGE

The 1960s were a time of rapid social change in the United States. Americans involved in the peace movement, the women's rights movement, and the African-American civil rights movement used fashion to push for change. Hippies grew their hair long and wore peace symbols to protest the war in Vietnam. Women wore pantsuits instead of skirts to show they could be equal to men in the workplace. Members of the Black Panther Party, an African-American civil rights organization, wore black berets, black gloves, and black leather jackets. Their military-style uniform showed they were strong, unified, and ready to fight for racial equality.

Black Power against oppression. For their action, Smith and Carlos were removed from the Olympic team and their medals were taken from them. But in this televised moment, a fashion statement brought the world's attention to the social struggle of African Americans.

From Ancient Egypt to the Future

Fashion in the Western world— that is, Europe, the Americas, and Australia—has a long history. The roots of European fashion can be found in ancient Egypt, where pharaohs were trendsetters, as well as ancient Greece and Rome. Travel and trade with other cultures brought new styles, materials, and techniques to clothing design. In later centuries, fashion changed quickly. Clothes went in and out of style with each cultural milestone. Fashions have been influenced by war, religion, social movements, and

At the 1968 Olympics, two US athletes wore black gloves to protest racism.

scientific discoveries. Some styles have been short-lived fads; others long-lasting trends.

Today's fashion continues to evolve as cutting-edge designers and trendsetting celebrities come up with unique twists on classic garments or push the boundaries to create outrageous new styles. Their efforts remind us that fashion is an art form. Designers don't just make clothes—they create moving, wearable art.

Chapter 2

Ancient Fashions that Amaze

$\mathcal{A}$pproximately 170,000 years ago, humans wrapped furs and skins around their bodies to protect themselves from freezing conditions following the second-to-last Ice Age.[1] These simple garments were some of the first items of clothing ever worn. Prehistoric peoples also fashioned clothing and jewelry out of grasses, leaves, bones, and shells.

Over time, people developed skills to create more sophisticated garments. They learned to weave fabrics from plant fibers and wool. They began sewing, joining pieces of fabric or animal skin by stitching them together with thread. Instead of simply draping over the body, clothing was designed to fit the human form. It was

Nefertiti, queen of Egypt in the 1300s BCE, was one of the world's first fashion icons.

made not only to protect people from the elements but also to enhance their appearance. Fashion was born.

Western fashion has its roots in the clothing styles of ancient Egypt, Greece, and Rome. Because clothing material deteriorates quickly, few examples of ancient clothing remain today. Fashion scholars must look to other sources, such as sculptures, paintings, and mosaics, to learn about the hairstyles, clothing, and other fashions worn in ancient times.

Fashion in Ancient Egypt

The civilization of ancient Egypt, located on the Nile River in northeastern Africa, flourished from approximately 3000 to 30 BCE. The pyramids weren't the only things the Egyptians created that had staying power. Egyptian burial practices preserved many articles of clothing for scholars to study. When the tomb of Pharaoh Tutankhamen, commonly known as King Tut, was opened in 1922, archaeologists discovered wooden chests filled with the young king's clothing, including loincloths, tunics, headdresses, and sandals worked in gold.[4] These articles of clothing probably represented the height of fashion in ancient Egypt. Unlike today, fashion in ancient times did not change very much. The same basic clothing styles were used for hundreds and even thousands of years.

Egyptians had to dress for extremely hot desert conditions. Because of this, their clothing was light, loose, and breathable. The most common fabric was linen, woven from the fibers of the flax plant. It was usually left in its natural color or bleached white in the sun. Egyptian women typically wore a *kalasiris*, a slim sheath dress formed in the shape of a tube. There were many variations on this garment. It could be belted with rope or held up with sleeves.

Wealthy women had more elaborate fashion options. Nefertiti, the wife of King Akhenaten, is

DECODING FASHION THROUGH MODERN SCIENCE

Modern technologies allow scientists to examine ancient fashions in a new light. For example, scientific tests examining metal wear and residue showed that decorative rings found in the tomb of Egyptian queen Amanishakheto were worn not on her fingers, as expected, but in her hair. The Carbon-14 dating process can be used to determine the age of ancient clothing items, such as linen shirts found in ancient Egyptian tombs.

This illustration shows an Egyptian woman in a *kalasiris* and a man in a *schenti*. The headdresses identify them as royalty.

depicted in ancient artwork wearing long, flowing linen gowns with crisp pleats. Starched or pleated clothing was something only very wealthy women could wear. Keeping the fabric clean and pressed required the work of domestic slaves.

Egyptian men went bare chested and wore a kilt-like garment called a *schenti* that wrapped around the hips. Different variations existed for the different classes.

Common laborers wore schenti made of leather or coarse cloth, while light linen was favored by the wealthy. Pharaohs sometimes wore decorative belts over their schenti from which lions' tails were hung. Striped or colored schenti were worn by soldiers.

Egyptian Accessories, Makeup, and Wigs

Jewelry worn by wealthy Egyptians included gold necklaces, collars, bracelets, and anklets inlaid with rough natural stones, such as lapis lazuli, turquoise, and feldspar. Royals wore a striped headscarf called a *klaft*. The image of King Tut on his sarcophagus shows him wearing this accessory.

Living in a hot climate, personal hygiene was extremely important to the ancient Egyptians. Bathing rituals involved scrubbing, perfuming, and shaving the skin. Because long hair was uncomfortable in the heat and attracted head lice, wealthy men and women shaved their heads and wore wigs dyed jet black.

Egyptian men were clean-shaven, but rulers sometimes wore fake beards. Called postiches, these metal beards were attached with a ribbon that tied over the head.

Both men and women wore makeup. They applied thick lines of dark kohl around the eyes to create a dramatic almond shape. The kohl had a practical purpose, as it reduced the glare of the sun and helped prevent eye infections. They also wore green eye paint made from copper and colored their lips with red and purple pigments.

Ancient Greek Style

The ancient Greek civilization (800 BCE to 600 CE) grew into an empire that ruled the Mediterranean region. The art, architecture, government, and philosophy of classical Greek culture laid the foundations for Western civilization.

When it came to ancient Greek fashion, comfort and simplicity ruled. Both men and women wore a garment called a chiton. This was a long, sleeveless shirt made of a rectangular piece of wool or linen sewn up the sides and fastened at the shoulders. The chiton was often brightly colored or patterned and could be cinched at the waist with a belt or girdle. Women commonly wore a version of the chiton called a peplos. The peplos was folded over at the top and draped down, giving the appearance of a shorter tunic worn over a longer one.

Ancient Greek art reveals fashion of the time, such as this carving of the Greek goddess Athena wearing a peplos.

A cape called a himation was often worn over the chiton. This was a rectangle of fabric that draped over the shoulders and sometimes wrapped around the torso. Over time, the himation grew longer and more elaborate. It eventually reached up to 12 feet (4 m) long and was worn elegantly draped around the body.[5] Leather sandals were the most common footwear.

Greek men and women wore perfumes made from flowers and spices. Women moisturized their skin and removed body hair. Since pale skin was considered a sign of status and beauty, wealthy Greek women used white makeup made from lead. Although they did not realize it at the time, the lead in their makeup was toxic. It caused sores and blemishes that needed to be covered up with even more makeup. Over time, lead poisoning could even be fatal.

Hair had symbolic meaning for the ancient Greeks. Both men and women wore long hair, cutting it only when in mourning or in special rites of passage. A bride's hair was cut on her wedding day, and a lock was offered to the goddesses. In Athens, boys cut

A Deadly Beauty Routine

For ancient Greek and Roman women, tanned skin was considered low class, the sign of a laborer who had to work outdoors in the sun. Extremely white skin was the ideal. Women painted their faces with white makeup to achieve a pale complexion. Although they did not realize it, this beauty routine was deadly. The makeup contained lead, a toxic metal. It caused blemishes and sores and could even lead to facial paralysis and death. But since the ill effects came after years of use, people did not realize how dangerous the makeup was. European women continued to use white lead makeup for hundreds of years. When the cosmetics industry was regulated in the early 1900s, toxic ingredients such as lead, mercury, and arsenic were banned.

their hair at puberty and offered the cut hair to the gods. They let it grow long again when they reached manhood. In the classical period, beginning in approximately 500 BCE, short hair became fashionable for men.[6]

Men and women curled and braided their long hair and dyed it using plant dyes. Blond was the favored color, achieved by washing the hair with yellow flowers or applying bleach made from wood ash. Creative Greeks occasionally colored their hair white, black, gold, red, or even pale blue.

Fashions in Ancient Rome

Classical Greek culture powerfully influenced the civilization of ancient Rome, which originated in the Italian peninsula. From approximately 27 BCE until 476 CE, the Roman Empire ruled the Mediterranean. The empire stretched from Great Britain to Turkey and included parts of northern Africa. Romans traded with and fought against peoples all over Europe, Asia, and Africa. Because of this, their fashions reflected both Eastern and Western trends.

During the time of the Roman Empire, Roman women and men wore comfortable, draped clothing, similar to the Greek style. Women tended to wear lightweight fabrics, such as cotton and linen, purchased through the empire's extensive trade network with India and Egypt. Wealthy women wore expensive fabrics, such as Chinese silk in bright yellow, deep blue, red, pink, or light green. Men wore more subdued colors and heavier, denser fabrics.

For women, the most common garment was the stola, a long dress with or without sleeves, belted below the bust and at the hips. A short cape called an *olicula* could be worn over the stola for warmth.

The tunic and toga were the standard articles of clothing for men. The tunic, similar to the Greek chiton, was a simple shirt made from two rectangular pieces of cloth, with slits for armholes. It was usually belted at the waist. A toga, a draped garment made from a piece of rectangular or oval-shaped fabric, was worn over the tunic. Togas were a mark of status. They could be worn only by male citizens of Rome—not by women, foreigners, or slaves. The drape and color of a man's tunic and toga showed his rank and occupation. For example, the ruling class of senators wore a tunic with wide purple stripes at the shoulders.

The Toga

The toga was an important marker of social, political, and economic status during the Roman Empire. Only Roman citizens were allowed to wear them. In its early days, the toga was made from a small piece of rectangular or oval-shaped fabric and draped around the body over a tunic or loincloth. However, as time went on, the toga became bigger and more elaborate. Some were up to 18 feet (5.5 m) long and 11.5 feet (3.5 m) wide.[7] Very wealthy Romans wore such enormous togas they required slaves to help them dress.

Roman Skincare, Hair, and Jewelry

Some Roman beauty rituals might be considered unappealing today. For example, sheep fat mixed with milk and breadcrumbs was applied to the face to improve the complexion. Not surprisingly, this mixture often smelled very bad after a few hours! Like the Greeks, Roman women used lead-based white makeup on their faces. They occasionally tinted the mixture with wine to make their cheeks pink. Soot was rubbed onto the eyebrows and eyelashes to make them black.

Roman men wore their hair short and were clean-shaven. Being bald was considered unattractive, so they combed their hair forward to cover bald spots. Wealthy women curled their hair in elaborate styles and wore wigs.

Royal Purple

During the Roman Empire and in later centuries, the color purple was reserved for rulers and the very wealthy. This was because purple dye was extremely difficult to produce, and was therefore very expensive. Tyrian purple, a color created in the city of Tyre (in modern-day Lebanon), was especially coveted. In order to make one gram of dye, laborers had to collect more than 9,000 sea snail shells, suffer a terribly foul smell as they boiled the shells for days in lead pots, and finally spend hours crushing the shells to create a fine purple powder.[8] Fabrics colored with Tyrian purple were often worth their weight in gold!

A common article of jewelry for both men and women in both ancient Greece and Rome was the fibula, a brooch used to fasten clothing. Metals including gold, silver, iron, and copper were hammered into delicate shapes for necklaces, earrings, rings, and bracelets. As the empire expanded, jewelry was set with precious stones such as diamonds, emeralds, sapphires, and pearls from Egypt.

Glamour in Byzantium

The western Roman Empire fell in 476 CE after invasions by Germanic tribes. The eastern city of Byzantium (modern-day Istanbul, Turkey), renamed Constantinople, became the new capital city. The Roman Empire during this time is called the Byzantine Empire (330 CE to 1452 CE). Christianity was the official state religion. The church had an extremely powerful influence on culture, dictating what was appropriate for people to wear.

By the 500s CE, the traditional Roman toga was worn by government officials only.[9] Christian values meant that both women and men dressed modestly, wearing layered clothing that hid their bodies. A common outfit for women included a long, tight

Christianity influenced Byzantine fashion. This mosaic from Ravenna, Italy, shows Emperor Justinian wearing jewels and brocade, surrounded by religious men in plain robes.

chemise, a slip-like undergarment, under a shorter tunic. Over this, women often added a Roman stola and a veil covering the head and shoulders. Men wore baggy pantaloons or knee-length breeches over wool hose. On top, they wore a dalmatic, a tunic with long, wide sleeves. A shorter tunic was worn over that, along with a wide, long cloak that draped over the shoulders.

Byzantine clothing was richly decorated. Jewelry was heavy and intricate, set with precious stones. Pearls were especially prized, since they were rare and hard to find. Enameling, a jewelry-making technique from Greece and Persia, was popular. Jewelers used wire to craft delicate scenes and patterns, then filled the space between with brightly colored enamel. Golden crosses reflected the importance of Christianity.

Emperor Justinian, who ruled from 527 to 565 CE, and his wife Theodora wore imported silks brocaded with gold and silver thread and embellished with jewels. The upper classes imitated Justinian and Theodora, whose tastes in clothing influenced the entire region for centuries.

Fashions worn in ancient Egypt, Greece, Rome, and Byzantium were all notable for their function, beauty, and symbolism. However, the same outfits were in style for hundreds or thousands of years. As history marched on, fashion would evolve at a much faster pace.

THE SECRET OF SILK: A PRECIOUS FABRIC

Silk made in China was one of the most precious textiles in the ancient world. The soft, shiny fabric was made from fibers extracted from the silkworm. Europeans loved the luxurious and expensive fabric but did not know how it was made. In approximately 552 to 563 CE, Byzantine emperor Justinian sent monks to China as spies.[10] They stole silkworms and smuggled them back to Constantinople. Soon the Byzantines were making their own silk.

Chapter 3

Fashions of the Middle Ages

$\mathcal{E}$urope entered the Middle Ages, also known as the medieval period, around 500 CE. Lasting until approximately 1500, this period saw the rise of a new social order that included knights, nobles, and powerful monarchs; a sweeping and devastating plague that forever changed Europe; and some of the most delightful, beautiful, and odd fashions ever worn. Despite all the cultural and social transitions that occurred between the dawn of the Byzantine Era and the end of the Middle Ages, one thing stayed the same: the Christian Church remained a powerful social and cultural influence.

A medieval knight, queen, and lady.
The knight wears fashionably pointed shoes.

Fashion for Christian Modesty

The influence of the church during the Middle Ages meant both men and women dressed modestly, since any display of skin was considered a sign of poor morals. Clothing was loose and layered to hide the shape of the body. Both men and women wore long, flowing gowns over long-sleeved tunics. Over this, they wore a short overtunic belted at the waist. A vest or cloak could be added for warmth. Married women covered their hair and neckline with veils and headdresses.

The use of makeup was considered immoral. The ideal look for women was a pale face with very thin, almost invisible eyelashes and eyebrows. Women

Eastern Style: Crusades and Marco Polo

Starting in 1095 and lasting throughout the Middle Ages, the Roman Catholic Church backed a series of wars called the Crusades to restore Christianity in sites it considered holy in and around Jerusalem. Soldiers fighting in the Crusades were exposed to Eastern culture, traditions, and fashions. When the Italian trader and explorer Marco Polo (1254–1324) made his famous and pioneering trek across Asia, he brought back many items of Eastern fashion.

Soon, European wardrobes had an Eastern flair. In addition to the colored and embroidered silks from China, velvet was introduced from Asia. The wimple, a headscarf that draped under the chin, was adapted from headscarves worn by Muslim women. Pointed shoes modeled after Asian slippers became a trend for men.

Portrait of a Young Woman, by Rogier van der Weyden,
ca. 1445, shows a lady wearing a wimple.

used extreme measures to achieve this look. They
applied leeches to their faces to drain the blood and
shaved, plucked, and bleached their brows and lashes.
By the 1300s, a high forehead became fashionable, so
women plucked and shaved the hair along their hairlines.

Women's hair was long, often tied up in braids or
a low knot called a chignon. They also curled their
hair and threaded it with colorful ribbons. Beards,

An illustration from 1300s France shows a peasant herding pigs. His plain robe and leggings would have been made of coarse fabric to be durable in winter and summer.

mustaches, and long, flowing hair for men were discouraged by the church. Clergy instructed faithful Christian men to keep their faces clean-shaven and their hair short. Popular styles for men included the bowl cut and the longer pageboy, worn with bangs and parted in the middle.

During the late Middle Ages, clothing became less conservative. Women's dresses became tighter in the waist, arms, and hips. Men began wearing short gowns paired with hose. On top, they added a short, tight-fitting jacket called a doublet. Bright colors were fashionable. A parti-colored look, with contrasting colors on each half of a garment, became trendy in the 1300s.

Peasants, Nobles, and Royalty

A gulf existed between the wealthy and the poor during the Middle Ages. Kings, queens, nobles, knights, and high-ranking clergy held all the land and power. They occupied a privileged place in society, and the

Extreme Fashions of the Black Plague

In 1347, a devastating epidemic of bubonic plague, known as the Black Death, struck Europe. An estimated 75 to 200 million people died.[1] As is common in difficult times, fashion was a distraction. Clothing became more flamboyant. Tight bodices, raised hemlines that revealed the ankles, and jagged decorative stitching were popular styles in women's clothing. Other extreme fashions included long, pointed shoes for men and tall headdresses for women. The pointed shoes, called *cracowes* or *poulaines*, were inspired by Asian slippers. The tips of the shoes became so long Edward III of England issued laws restricting their length. They could extend anywhere from a few inches to two feet (0.6 m).[2] The cone-shaped *hennin* was a veiled hat popular in the 1400s in France. Wealthy women could wear towering versions up to four feet (1.2 m) tall.[3]

common people, the peasants, had to serve them. This social order was reflected in the way people dressed.

Most peasants were laborers and farmers. They wore tough and durable material, such as wool, linen, fur, and sheepskin. The typical outfit was a long tunic under a shorter overtunic, with a cloak in winter. Men sometimes wore their tunics shorter with leggings underneath to make their clothing more practical for work. Their clothing was usually natural gray and brown, or colored green or blue with plant dyes.

Unlike commoners, wealthy people could afford multiple items of clothing for different occasions. In contrast to the drab, rough fabrics worn by peasants, the rich wore brightly colored silks and velvets embroidered with gold thread and decorated with gold, pearls, and precious stones. Professional tailors started to appear during the 1300s, allowing the wealthy to have clothing specially made to fit their bodies.[4] For the first time, lacing and buttons were used to fasten clothing. This

Buttons used to fasten clothing first appeared in Europe in the 1200s.[5] They allowed clothes to be fitted to the body rather than draped.

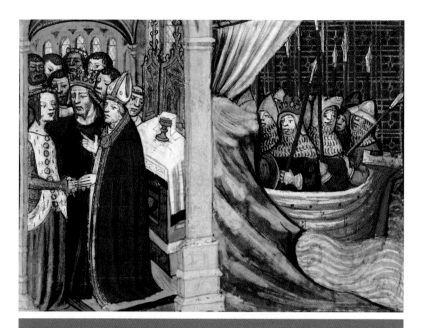

At left, Eleanor of Aquitaine and Louis VII of France wear purple robes at their wedding in 1137. *At right,* Louis and his soldiers wear chain mail hoods as they leave for war in 1147.

meant that unlike earlier styles, which were draped and belted, clothing was more fitted.

Eleanor of Aquitaine was queen of France from 1137 to 1152 and queen of England from 1154 to 1189. Wealthy Europeans imitated Eleanor's colorful and luxurious style. Under her influence, gowns became more fitted in the bodice and were worn with decorative belts and fur-trimmed cuffs. Skirts were cut wide, with large amounts of rich fabric that fell in folds down to the floor, hiding the feet. Sleeves were so dramatically long they dragged on the ground.

Knights and the Clergy

Knights were noble warriors in service to the king and Church. Becoming a knight was a great honor and achievement. Knights began their training during childhood, learning how to fight, hunt, and ride. They also learned poetry and intellectual games, such as chess. Knights were often finely dressed. A suit of armor was worn for tournaments, battles, and ceremonies. Early armor was made from links of steel called chain mail. By the 1200s, plates of metal were used.[6] Suits of armor covered most of a man's body. While they protected from deadly axes, spears, and arrows, they were very bulky and made movement difficult.

Bishops, cardinals, and other high-ranking clergy wore elegant embroidered robes and tunics, while priests wore simple black robes. These religious vestments are still worn by the clergy today. Knights and clergy often shaved their hair in a practice called tonsure. A common style was to shave a circle at the top of the head, leaving a ring of hair all around. This hairstyle, like so many other aspects of medieval fashion, showed humility and devotion to God.

Knights and Heraldry

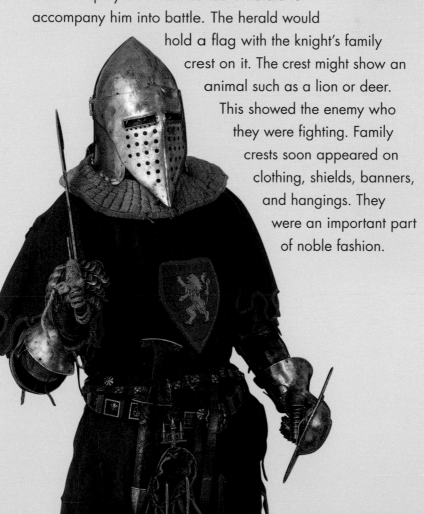

During the Middle Ages, the wearing of family crests became popular. Since a knight's armor concealed the face, a heraldic symbol allowed others to identify him in battle. This tradition began as a way to identify combatants in battle. A knight would employ a servant called a herald to accompany him into battle. The herald would hold a flag with the knight's family crest on it. The crest might show an animal such as a lion or deer. This showed the enemy who they were fighting. Family crests soon appeared on clothing, shields, banners, and hangings. They were an important part of noble fashion.

Chapter 4

The Renaissance: A Fashion Rebirth

$\mathcal{A}$s the Middle Ages came to a close, Europe experienced a period called the Renaissance, "rebirth." During this period, from approximately the 1400s until the 1600s, a new emphasis on art, science, literature, and music dominated the lives of the upper classes. Scholars looked to the future while also embracing the art and writings of the ancient Greek and Roman masters. While the Renaissance affected people living in all corners of Europe, its epicenters were the cities of Florence, Rome, and Venice in Italy and Flanders in Belgium.

The ideals of the Renaissance included a new emphasis on self-awareness. This showed in the way

Renaissance fashions worn by Italian noblewoman Catherine de Medici (Queen of France from 1547 to 1559) and John of Austria

people dressed themselves. Instead of being reserved for the very wealthy, fashion was also embraced by a new economic group called the middle classes. Made up of merchants and tradespeople, the middle class was a group of people who earned enough money to support themselves and their families and had some left over to buy nonnecessities. The emergence of the middle class meant many different types of people were wearing, experimenting with, and affecting fashion trends.

During this time period, travel became faster, easier, and more accessible for the middle classes. Because of this, trends spread through Europe quickly. Luxury goods were traded with relative ease and people began adopting the styles worn in distant lands as their own.

Corsets

Corsets, or stays, emerged as an important part of a woman's wardrobe during the Renaissance. These tight-fitting undergarments cinched in a woman's waist to make it very narrow, while pressing her bust forward and up. Corsets were constructed from durable fabric and reinforced with whalebone, reed, or metal. Laces in the back allowed them to be loosened or tightened. Noble women wore their corsets very tight in order to look as fashionable as possible. A fine lady was not expected to work or participate in rough physical activity. Peasant women, on the other hand, had to keep their corsets rather loose in order to work and move freely throughout the day.

Renaissance Fashion: Emphasis on Form and Shape

Clothing for women had been relatively modest during the Middle Ages. Dresses billowed loosely over the body. But by the end of the 1400s, dresses were structured to mold a woman's shape. Gowns featured low, V-shaped waistlines. Tight corsets and stiff triangles of fabric called stomachers held in the waist and abdomen. A new invention called the farthingale was worn under the skirt to give it a wide shape, further emphasizing a small waist. First worn in Spain, the farthingale was a set of wooden, reed, or whalebone hoops worn under or sewn into a skirt. Making skirts to cover the farthingale required huge amounts of fabric, which made this style very expensive.

Like women's clothing, men's clothing exaggerated the shape of the body. The chest and shoulders were

THE CHANGING FEMALE SILHOUETTE

A silhouette is the general shape or outline of a body. Over time, many different female silhouettes have been popular. During the Middle Ages, a rounded stomach was in style, while during the Renaissance, a fashionable silhouette included a narrow waist and wide hips, created with the help of a stomacher, corset, and farthingale. Padded sleeves made the shoulders wide, furthering the illusion of a tiny waist.

Renaissance
Men's Fashion

For a wealthy male, a typical outfit consisted of the following items:

Jerkin: An outer jacket (not shown here) that was usually left open at the front to show the doublet.

Doublet: A short, tight jacket, padded to give the wearer extra bulk at the chest and shoulders.

Shirt: A crisp white linen shirt. This garment required careful cleaning and pressing, and was therefore a sign of great wealth.

Codpiece: A triangular piece of padding that both covered and emphasized a man's crotch. These could be quilted, brightly colored, and even jeweled. Some even had pockets. Henry VIII of England was said to have stored money in his.

Breeches, or Upper Hose: Short pants worn over stockings, often padded or puffed.

Stockings, or Lower Hose: High socks that were often attached at the knee with garters.

Doublet

Shirt

Codpiece

Breeches

Stockings

made to look very broad and masculine while the waist was made as small as possible. To achieve this look, men wore puffed sleeves and padded their chests and shoulders with hay. Tight stockings and hose made the waist and legs look narrow. Bright colors were popular, especially for younger men. Patterns, stripes, squares, and patches made these bright clothes even more flamboyant.

Renaissance Makeup, Hair, and Accessories

As in the Middle Ages, extremely white skin, a high forehead, and delicate eyebrows were the ideal look. Women plucked and shaved their brows and hairline and lightened the skin on their faces.

Unaware of how toxic it was, women still used white lead-based makeups on their faces, and continued to do so throughout the 1600s and 1700s. To contrast their pallid skin, women applied beauty marks, small patches made of black velvet or taffeta. Patches were also useful in covering facial scars caused by smallpox, an infectious disease that caused sores on the skin. A popular accessory grew from the use of face patches: ornate and delicate boxes for holding spare beauty marks.

Renaissance women wore their hair in elaborate, fancy styles, braided, curled, or in combination with false hairpieces. Some wore wigs. Many men and women used natural pigments and vinegars to dye their hair different colors, but blond was the most popular choice. Various types of hoods and bonnets emphasized the high forehead.

Royal Style Icons

Many royals became style icons of the Renaissance. Charles V of Spain and the Netherlands was famous for his luxurious fashions. He was known to wear a doublet made from silver brocade along with a gold robe lined with fur. Francois I of France wore a suit of armor plated with gold. In Italy, the ruling Medici family in Florence set styles that were copied all over Europe. Fashion in Italy was also influenced by the Italian painters,

Queen Elizabeth I is said to have suffered from lead poisoning caused by her habitual use of white lead face cream.

Elizabeth I of England was a style icon of the Renaissance. Her high forehead, pale skin, and stiff neck ruff were the height of fashion.

including Michelangelo, Leonardo da Vinci, Raphael, and Botticelli.

In England, the ruling Tudor family set fashions. King Henry VIII, who ruled from 1509 to 1547 and famously had six wives, was also known for his sense of style. Portraits show his opulent, brocaded costumes encrusted with precious stones and trimmed with fur. Elizabeth I, Henry's daughter by Anne Boleyn, reigned from 1558 to 1603, a period known as the Elizabethan era. Her pale skin, high forehead, and red hair were ideals of beauty. One famous hairstyle featured two puffs that framed her face like a heart.

Elizabeth I was especially famous for wearing a large ruff. It was a piece of stiff, often pleated, linen or gauze that stood up like a very high collar around the neckline. Both men and women wore ruffs during the Renaissance. They required the wearer to stand very straight with the head held high. This unnatural posture was only possible for the very wealthy, who did not need to work or move much during the day.

Hats, Headdresses, and Beheadings

Hats and headdresses were popular during the Renaissance. Peasant men wore simple caps and straw hats to shield their faces from the sun. Noble men wore a wide variety of headwear, from berets to wide-brimmed hats with fancy trim, such as feathers or ribbons.

Renaissance women enjoyed styles of headwear from different parts of Europe. Henry VIII's first wife, Catherine of Aragon, wore the English Gable headdress, or Spanish hood. It rose to a peak at the crown of her head and fell down to her jawline. His second bride, the glamorous Anne Boleyn, wore a headdress called the French hood. This was a more revealing style, worn farther back on the head to show the hairline. When Anne was beheaded for crimes of indecency, people quickly stopped wearing the French hood for fear of being associated with the dead queen.

Style for All

Most people living during the Renaissance could not dress like royalty. Even if they could afford it, laws prohibited common people from wearing certain colors and fabrics. For instance, in a 1574 law, Elizabeth I specified that purple silk and sable fur could be worn only by the queen, king, and family members.[1] Red velvet was only for the highest nobility. Many other fabrics, too, were restricted to nobles. Those who dared violate the law could be fined and publicly humiliated by having their clothes torn from their bodies.

Still, the Renaissance did mark a period when fashionable clothing was accessible to larger numbers of people. New technologies in weaving and increased trade made fabric more affordable for middle-class buyers. Since women's clothing was sold in pieces, middle-class ladies could keep up with the latest fashion by buying just part of an outfit and swapping it out. For instance, a skirt, bodice, and sleeves were sold separately, allowing a woman to buy a more fashionable bodice to wear with last year's skirt and sleeves. Fashions became more personalized, paving the way for the exciting fashion trends that were about to emerge.

Chapter 5

From Opulence to Revolution

*D*uring the 1600s and 1700s, the center of fashion moved from Italy and Belgium to France. Louis XIV, also known as the Sun King, ruled France from 1643 to 1715. He and his court were famous for their lavish clothing. All around Europe, people tried to imitate the glamorous fashions of the French court.

In England, civil war (1642–1646) interrupted the luxurious life of the royals, ending with the execution of Charles I. Fashions were austere during the period from 1649 to 1660, when Oliver Cromwell, a Puritan, was head of the English government. The crowning of Charles II in 1660 marked the Restoration of the English throne. Charles II, who had been living in exile in

Marie Antoinette, wife of French King Louis XVI, came to symbolize the over-the-top fashions of the French court.

MARIE ANTOINETTE, THE QUEEN OF FASHION

Marie Antoinette, wife of Louis XVI, was the queen of France from 1774 to 1793. She had expensive tastes and preferred luxurious fashions. In fact, one woman at court claimed she preferred to be called the queen of fashion rather than the queen of France. At the time, most French people struggled just to buy enough food to eat. Marie Antoinette was seen as an example of royal extravagance. She was executed with a guillotine by the revolutionary government when she was just 37.

France, brought French fashion home to England and ushered in a new era of English style.

As European powers settled the New World, high fashions of Europe traveled across the sea to British, French, and Spanish colonies in North and South America. Rich men and women from Charleston, South Carolina, to Buenos Aires, Argentina, could be seen at balls wearing the same glamorous styles that were popular in Paris and London, including powdered wigs, silk jackets, and embroidered cloth.

Lavish clothing, architecture, and art continued to flourish during the reign of Louis XV (1723–1724) and Louis XVI (1774–1793). Finally the French masses, tired of the enormous gap between the rich and poor, revolted. From 1787 to 1799, the French Revolution saw the execution of French royals and nobles via the guillotine. Suddenly decadent fashions fizzled and modest styles became popular.

Women's Styles: A Wider and Softer Silhouette

Women's fashions of the 1600s and 1700s were extremely decorative and multilayered. Clothing was trimmed with bows, ruffles, embroidery, lace, sashes, and fabric flowers. In place of the ruff, dresses featured a plunging neckline called a décolletage.

By the 1620s, the trend of the wide farthingale hoopskirt had faded and was replaced by a softer shape made with layers of petticoats, or underskirts. In the 1700s, a new silhouette emerged. Women created a wide, square skirt with the use of panniers, breadbasket-shaped pads worn on the hips. Eventually this trend became so extreme that some women's panniers made their hips five feet (1.5 m) wide![1]

Wigs and Pompadours

People of all classes wore wigs in the 1700s. Men wore a variety of styles, from full, long wigs that draped over the shoulders to curled styles tied back in a ponytail. Women often wore their hair in a pompadour, a powdered pouf with curls hanging down at the sides. The style got its name from Madame de Pompadour, mistress of King Louis XV. In the second half of the 1700s, hair grew taller and more elaborate. In a hairstyle called the pouf au sentiment, butterflies, birds, and twigs could be seen peeking out of a woman's fake tower of hair.

Baroque
and Rococo

Fashions of the 1600s and early 1700s are often called baroque. Baroque fashions were grand and dramatic, with flowing silks, gold embroidery, and layers of lace. Louis XIV of France, *shown below*, decorated his palace at Versailles in an ornate baroque style. A lighter, more playful style called rococo emerged in the mid-1700s. Floral patterns, bows, frills, and ruffles, and fanciful hairdos worn by Marie Antoinette were typical of rococo style. At the end of the century, these over-the-top fashions were replaced with a simple, classical style.

Men's Fashions: Heels, Wigs, and Three-Piece Suits

Louis XIV of France influenced men's fashions all around Europe. Rather short in stature at five feet three inches (1.6 m), he made himself look taller by wearing high heels and tall, curled wigs. Heels and wigs, along with ribbons and lace, became fashionable for both men and women. Knee-length waistcoats took the place of the shorter doublet. Waistcoats were sometimes embroidered with delicate images of animals or flowers or made from brightly colored silk or velvet.

In England, Charles II popularized a three-piece suit, influenced by styles worn in Persia. Made of a coat, waistcoat, and knee-length breeches, this is often considered the foundation for the modern men's suit. Early versions of this suit were made from dark English wool.

Revolution and Aftermath

During the French Revolution, peasant women showed their political beliefs with their clothing. Those who supported the revolution wore red, white, and blue clothing. Supporters of the royals wore black.

Simpler clothing was fashionable in the late 1700s. George Washington, later the first US president, wears a simple coat, waistcoat, and breeches in this portrait from 1776.

After the French Revolution, fashions became simpler and more modest. The lavish clothes that were popular before the revolution were not only out of style—they were dangerous. The wealthy feared the wrath of angry mobs, who had just beheaded many of their noble friends. Though this was most keenly felt in France, the shockwaves from the French Revolution were felt in all parts of Europe.

The glamour of Versailles and the ostentatious displays of wealth favored by royal courts would never again be matched. The world was gearing up for a new kind of revolution, and no one had time for bows and lace.

The Puritans

In stark contrast to baroque and rococo fashions were the somber styles of the English Puritans. This group of Christians wore somber styles with very little decoration. Black clothing with wide, white collars was a typical style, brought to colonial America by Pilgrim settlers in 1620. Puritan style influenced England the most during the period of the Commonwealth, from 1649 to 1660, when Oliver Cromwell was head of the English government. Conservative Puritan values continued to affect both English and American culture and fashion for centuries to come.

Chapter 6

Fashions for a Brand New World

The 1800s were a time of innovation in science and technology in Europe and the United States. This century saw the invention of the light bulb, the telephone, and the steam engine. The advances of the Industrial Revolution (1760–1840) continued to make production of all types of goods faster and more mechanized. In 1846, Isaac Singer introduced the first successful sewing machine for garment factories. Before long, knitting machines started appearing in clothing shops. These made the production of garments such as elastic stockings and gloves fast and easy.

Shortly after the French Revolution, shops in Paris began selling prêt-à-porter, or ready-to-wear, clothing.

Queen Victoria and her husband, Prince Albert, set fashions for the 1800s and the Victorian Era (1837 to 1901).

FASHION MAGAZINES

Popular fashion magazines included *The Englishwoman's Domestic Magazine, Godey's Lady's Book, Peterson's,* and *La Belle Assemblée.* They featured short articles, sheet music, and fashion plates, which were full-page illustrations showing the newest styles. Many magazines also included patterns for women to make their own clothing after the latest fashion.

Garments were created in distinct sizes, rather than sewn to fit an individual's body. Now people could buy clothing off the rack, rather than having to be measured and then waiting for the clothes to be made. By the mid-1800s, shopping became a popular pastime all over Europe. Before long, the first department stores appeared. These allowed shoppers to browse many different items of finished clothing under one roof.

By 1889, sewing machines were sold for use in the home. Clothing patterns were sold through the mail. American tailor Ebenezer Butterick made his patterns from tissue paper. The paper could be laid over fabric to show where it needed to be cut and sewn. With sewing machines and easy-to-use patterns, professional and private tailors and dressmakers could make many popular fashions in a relatively short amount of time. Fashion was more accessible than ever.

Europe, especially Paris, was still considered the center of the fashion world in the 1800s. Women in the United States, Canada, and other parts of the globe relied on magazines to learn about the latest European styles.

Women's Fashions: Wider Skirts and Tighter Corsets

In the late 1700s and early 1800s, fashion saw a return to the flowing, easy classical styles of ancient Greece and Rome. Dresses featured a high waistline fitted just under the bust, similar to a belted chiton. This style was known as an Empire waist, after the glamorous Empress Josephine of France. The skirt flowed loosely, skimming the hips and legs, rather than being held out by starched petticoats. Hair was tied in ribbons rather than hidden

Charles Worth: Father of Haute Couture

Charles Worth was an English designer often called the father of haute couture—French for "high fashion." Worth designed clothing for royalty, aristocrats, and celebrities from the United States and Europe in the mid-1800s. Following the traditional role of a tailor, he created fine, hand-sewn garments for clients based on their measurements. However, in an innovative twist, he also created entire collections of clothing to sell to his wealthy clients in his Paris studio, Maison Worth, which opened in 1858. Glamorous women flocked to Maison Worth to view his creations on live models in fashion shows. Worth's most famous client was Empress Eugénie of France.

A fashion plate issued by Butterick shows the bustled skirts popular in the 1870s.

under bonnets and hats, and arms were left bare, a shocking thing at the time.

By the 1820s, women were back to wearing tight-fitting tubular corsets under their stiff, structured gowns. Puffed sleeves soon came into style. By the 1830s, sleeves had become so enormously puffed that women could not fit them inside their coat sleeves. Capes and cloaks became a fashionable way to stay warm.

Skirts again began to grow in volume in the 1850s. In order to achieve the popular full look, women were wearing up to six petticoats under their skirts. The layers were so heavy they made it hard to move. As a solution, the American inventor W. S. Thompson created the cage crinoline. This was a lightweight frame made of metal hoops, worn under the skirt. Later, in the 1870s, it was replaced by the bustle, a small pillow or set of hoops worn on a woman's backside. It pushed a woman's skirt up and out at the back, while allowing the fabric to hang straight down in the front. Empress Eugénie, wife of Napoleon III of France (who ruled from 1853 to 1871), made this style popular.

Corsets:
An Unhealthy Fashion

Corsets were worn throughout the 1800s. The use of corsets reflected women's role in society. Tight corsets that restricted movement emphasized that women were the weaker sex, dependent on men. While advertisers and fashion

CLOTHING AND WOMEN'S RIGHTS

Wide crinolines, puffed sleeves, and tight corsets restricted women's movement, hindering their ability to play sports or work. In 1851, women's rights activist Amelia Bloomer proposed a shocking new style for women: pants! The loose, full pantaloons, worn under a skirt, made sporting activities such as bicycling easier. Bloomer wrote about the pants in her newspaper, *The Lily*, sparking a fashion trend named after her. But the trend fizzled out when women wearing these "bloomers" were teased, mocked, and even physically attacked in public for daring to wear "men's clothing." It was not until the 1890s, when the bicycle became more popular, that bloomers became acceptable for women to use as sport clothing.

The S-bend corset created a unique silhouette.

designers argued the corset was necessary to develop a womanly figure, evidence suggested the corset was actually harmful to women's health. Worn tightly, it compressed the lungs and other internal organs and deformed the ribcage. As women started fighting for rights in the late 1800s, some stopped wearing corsets. Some of these "New Women" even wore an outfit similar to men's clothing—with a shirtwaist tucked into bloomers. This outfit made bicycling easier.

A new corset shape was introduced in the early 1900s. Advertised as a healthier alternative to the traditional version, this corset pushed the chest forward and the hips back. It reduced pressure on the lungs while still emphasizing a fashionably tiny "wasp" waist. Viewed from the side, women's bodies formed an S shape. Its distinct shape earned it the name the S-bend corset.

Men's Wear: Dandies in Dark Suits and Hats

English men's fashion in the 1800s was dark and understated. Bright silks and ruffles were out, and black became the favored color for men's formal suits, as it is today. Stylish men of the early 1800s were called dandies. These tastemakers wore expensive tailored clothing and took great pride in their appearance. A typical outfit was a crisp, clean shirt and vest and a dark dress jacket with tails, worn with light-colored breeches and riding boots. Top hats, neckties, canes, umbrellas, and pocket watches were popular accessories. Dandies

The well-dressed man of the 1800s wore a tailored jacket, vest, and trousers. A top hat, cane, and an elegant cravat tied at the neck completed the look.

were often ridiculed as being too feminine. Some even wore corsets to fit into their tight clothing.

With the introduction of ready-to-wear in the second half of the 1800s, men were more likely to buy their clothes off the rack rather than have them custom-fitted by a tailor. More casual, loose-fitting sack suits became popular. These were also known as ditto suits, since the same fabric was used for the jacket, waistcoat, and trousers. The casual style of the ditto suit did not match the sleek formality of the top hat. Soon, men began wearing a more rounded hat called a bowler. These were made in gray, black, white, and brown.

Hair and Makeup of the Victorian Era

The trend for long, curled hair and wigs for men, fashionable in previous centuries, was fading away by the beginning of the 1800s. Most men wore their hair short with a crisp side part. Some facial hair, such as a mustache or sideburns, was acceptable. However, many men chose to remain clean-shaven.

Women curled their hair and wore it in buns, braids, chignons, or piled on top of their heads. A trend that lasted for most of the century was to wear the hair parted in the middle with long curls hanging down by the ears.

Queen Victoria, who ruled England from 1837 to 1901, valued sensibility and strict morals and considered wearing makeup to be a sign of immodesty. Women throughout England began wearing more conservative clothing and less makeup in deference to their queen. In fact, the only women who continued to wear heavy makeup were actresses and prostitutes. The term *painted lady* arose in popular culture to refer to women of questionable morals.

Chapter 7

Beautiful Age to Wartime

The Triangle Shirtwaist Company, a garment factory in New York City, caught fire in 1911. There were few exits, and all were locked to prevent employees from sneaking out for breaks or stealing cloth. The fire hose was old and rotten, and it was of little use in battling the flames. Trapped on the upper floors, desperate workers leapt from windows to their death. Ultimately, 146 employees, most of them women, died due to the negligence of the factory owners.[1] After this, the International Ladies Garment Workers Union (ILGWU) fought for better working conditions.

Wars, women's rights, and the economy also impacted the fashion world. From 1914 to 1918, World

The new century would see increased rights for women
and usher in many fashion changes.

War I was fought in brutal battles across Europe, Asia, Africa, and the Middle East. In the first two decades of the century, women in many countries successfully campaigned for the vote. Then the US stock market crashed in 1929, causing a Great Depression that had impact worldwide. From 1939 to 1944, World War II was fought in Europe, Africa, and Asia.

These monumental events changed everything about the way people lived, worked, ate, and dressed. Women celebrated their newfound freedom by lopping off their long hair and ditching their corsets in favor of boyish flapper dresses. Military uniforms inspired fashions for men and women. The 1900s, it seemed, were off to a wild start.

The Belle Epoque: The Era of Beauty and Leisure

At the beginning of the century, both men and women enjoyed a

SHIRTWAIST BLOUSE

The shirtwaist, a blouse for women modeled after a man's dress shirt, was an important part of a woman's wardrobe in the late 1800s and early 1900s. Women wore the shirtwaist tucked into a skirt, allowing for ease of movement. The shirtwaist became a symbol of women's newfound independence as they went to work in factories and shops during the Industrial Revolution. By the early 1900s, shirtwaists were available in every color, and they were often embellished with lace trim or ruffles.

period in fashion called the Belle Epoque, meaning "beautiful age." Lasting from approximately 1900 until 1914, this was a time for the wealthy to wear outfits suited for leisure activities such as boating, swimming, playing tennis, and driving cars. Bicycles, invented in the previous century, suddenly appeared all over city and country roads.

Belle Epoque fashion allowed the very wealthy to express their artistic and decorative sides. For women, this meant dressing in extremely feminine styles. Over their corsets, wealthy women wore light-colored and loose-fitting dresses that belted at the waist. Straw hats with flowers or ribbons kept the sun out of their eyes and light, short jackets kept them warm on cool summer evenings.

The Hobble Skirt

In contrast to the wide, bell-shaped look of the 1800s, achieved with petticoats and crinolines, women in the 1910s favored narrow, form-fitting skirts. In 1911, French fashion designer Paul Poiret took this trend to an extreme with the hobble skirt. This style fit a woman's knees and ankles so narrowly that she could only take very small steps while wearing it. Though it was considered extremely glamorous, it was also the subject of many jokes. One postcard from 1911 read, "The Hobble Skirt: What's that? It's the speed-limit skirt!"[2]

FROM BATHING
Dresses to Swimsuits

Swimwear for women changed drastically between 1875 and 1927. From the 1870s through the early 1900s, women wore bloomers under a long, belted dress. This outfit was too bulky for actual swimming but necessary for modesty. In 1907, competitive swimmer Annette Kellerman was arrested in Boston for wearing a suit that showed her thighs! By the 1920s, as women became more active in outdoor sports and leisure, a fitted, knit suit became acceptable.

By the 1940s, women were often seen wearing a two-piece swimsuit. These suits were cut high on the waist and low on the leg to avoid showing the navel and bikini line. In this photo from the time, actress Rita Hayworth sports a bikini with a bandeau top and halter.

More revealing bikinis became acceptable beachwear in the 1960s. This photo shows actress Raquel Welch modeling a white bikini.

Rich men also wore comfortable, casual clothing during this time. They matched flat-brimmed straw boater hats with striped blazers and light-colored flannel pants.

Styles for the Working Woman

World War I brought changes for people living around the globe. Women who had never worked outside of the home suddenly found themselves earning money to support their families while their husbands were away. The way women dressed reflected their new active roles. Most people also had less money during the war, so cheap fabrics that could be constructed into simple garments became popular.

Women wore ankle-length skirts along with button-down blouses and short, fitted jackets. Leather shoes or lace-up boots with modest heels were sturdy and comfortable choices for footwear. This outfit was appropriate for many different occupations and allowed easy movement. Another common ensemble was a long tunic worn over an ankle-length skirt. This was later adapted into the iconic World War I nurse's uniform.

After the war ended, women's fashions became simpler and even more comfortable. Dresses hung in

Jazz dancers such as Josephine Baker set the trend for fringe, feathers, bright makeup, and closely cropped hair for young flappers who danced the Charleston.

a straight line from the shoulders to mid-calf. Women stopped wearing corsets in favor of more comfortable elastic girdles that minimized their curves. The hourglass and S-shaped silhouette of the past was gone. Now women wanted to appear boyish and thin.

This boyish silhouette was especially popular in the 1920s. Jazz was a huge sensation, and women wanted to be able to dance the Charleston and other active, athletic dances. They wore dresses with low waistlines and skirts made up of fringe, feathers, or strips of fabric, revealing more skin than ever. On their feet, they often wore flirty high-heeled sandals or peep-toe pumps. Women who embraced this daring trend were called flappers. They were the ultimate examples of fashionable, modern, and free women.

Making Fashions Last

The stock market crash brought the Roaring Twenties to a screeching halt. Women were forced to make do with old clothing. Anything they did buy had to be built to last. Durable, simple, and functional styles were popular. When World War II began, this practical atmosphere became even more prevalent.

Coco Chanel

French designer Coco Chanel (1883–1971) redefined fashion for women beginning in the last years of World War I. Unlike the frilly, corseted styles, Chanel's clothing was sporty and easy to move around in. Her designs, including crewneck sweaters and striped shirts, were inspired by the uniforms of French sailors. The fabric she used was wool jersey, a lightweight, stretchy material normally used only for undergarments and sportswear. Chanel's stylish but comfortable clothing was practical for European and American women, since they had to ride buses, trains, and bicycles. Chanel became a fashion icon. Women rushed to buy her suits, cardigans, and little black dresses.

Just as during World War I, women returned to the workplace in functional, comfortable clothing. However, a shortage of fabric meant clothing had to be very simply made from as little fabric as possible. Women wore jackets and simple blouses. On the bottom, they wore garments that let them bicycle to work, such as knee-length skirts and even pants.

Glamorous movie stars made women's pants popular in the mid-1930s. Before this, they were a rare sight, only occasionally seen on a daring sportswoman. Actress Katherine Hepburn loved wearing wide-legged pants in her personal life and even wore them in the film *The Philadelphia Story* (1940). Beach pajamas were an extremely popular style of woman's pants. They were comfortable, wide-legged pants women could pair with a light top or wear over a swimsuit. These durable styles remained in fashion until the end of the war.

Wartime Makeup

In sharp contrast to the Victorian era when cosmetics were subtle, if worn at all, women in the 1920s wore makeup that was designed to be noticed. Lipstick, rouge, mascara, and nail polish were all worn in bright, bold colors. Popularized by Jazz Age flappers and silent film stars, this trend made women excited about expressing themselves through their makeup.

During World War II, most cosmetics were in short supply—except for lipstick. It was decided that lipstick, the ultimate sign of femininity, helped wartime morale.

Menswear: T-Shirts and Baggy Trousers

Men returning from World War I had many comfortable fashion choices. Suit jackets fell to just past the hip and featured a wide lapel. Trousers were straight, baggy, and often cuffed at the bottom. Just as the flapper dress was designed for easy dancing, men's fashion at this time was also affected by dance trends. Men wanted to be able to move comfortably no matter what song was playing.

When World War II began, men again shipped off to fight. Their new uniforms featured a

The Bra Is Born

Corsets fell out of fashion during World War I. The metal usually used to construct them was needed for the war effort, and the exaggerated curves made by corsets didn't fit well under the new flapper styles. By the 1920s, a simple brassiere that flattened the chest became popular. When the boyish flapper figure fell out of fashion, a new version of the bra emerged. This contraption was called the Maiden Form. It had two cups and was sewn into dresses. It became so popular the company producing it eventually started selling the Maiden Form on its own as a must-have undergarment for all women.

groundbreaking item: a cotton undershirt called the T-shirt. Though it had been included in the US Navy uniform during World War I, the T-shirt didn't gain popularity until it was part of the standard issue uniform for all soldiers in World War II. These young men were commonly seen wearing uniform pants and just a T-shirt. When heartthrob Marlon Brando wore a T-shirt in the 1951 film *A Streetcar Named Desire*, the comfortable undergarment quickly became an acceptable top to wear in public.

Fashion in the first half of the 1900s swung from conservative to liberal and back again countless times. It survived wars, rations, and social and economic upheavals. Men and women had seen and survived changes in domestic roles, and they were ready to return to their comfort zones. The only question was, would fashion and society allow it?

Chapter 8

Anything Goes

The second half of the 1900s was packed with historical events of enormous importance. American schools were desegregated, and the civil rights movement encouraged people to look beyond race. Wars in Vietnam and Korea caused political unrest and sparked a peace movement in the United States and abroad. The Beatles, British youth style, and hippies took over the cultural scene. The economy soared and then tanked.

These monumental changes weren't just confined to American soil. Similar changes were occurring around the globe. And all along the way, fashion kept changing and evolving to fit each new event, movement, and

Model Twiggy represented mod 1960s style with a pixie haircut, fake eyelashes, and a minidress.

feeling. Clothing from 1950 to 2000 was bright, bold, fabulous, and fun.

The role of women and minorities changed dramatically during this time. Women, gays, lesbians, and people of color gained more freedom and rights. This change was reflected in fashion. Clothing from different cultures and for different lifestyles became acceptable in mainstream society. Fashion has always been a means of self-expression, but this was truer than ever in the late twentieth century, when "anything goes" became the only fashion rule.

Postwar Fashion: Home and Business

After World War II, women hung up their work uniforms and returned to the home. Dresses became softer and more feminine. In 1947, designer Christian Dior introduced the "New Look" for women, an hourglass figure achieved with a tight girdle, fitted bra, and a wide, bell-shaped skirt that fell to just below the knee. Women wore this look in feminine day dresses, paired with high-heeled shoes. The outfit told

Women in the 1950s often wore long, full skirts and high heels—even at home in the kitchen.

the world they had returned to the traditional role of a homemaker.

Most men of the 1950s returned to work wearing clothing that echoed the traditional roles of pre-war life. Dark suits with slim trousers were worn with crisp white shirts and narrow ties. The look was businesslike and refined.

In the 1950s, teenagers for the first time had clothing that was distinct from their parents' styles. The booming economy and the rise of the automobile gave them more independence than ever before. Teen clothing was casual, fun, and rebellious. Teen girls

TWIGGY AND THE RISE OF THE SUPERMODEL

Lesley Hornby, nicknamed Twiggy, was one of the first supermodels. At just five feet six inches (1.7 m) and with a scrawny figure, she did not look anything like the curvy, tall models of her time.[1] But that didn't stop her from becoming the most famous model of the 1960s. By the 1990s, supermodels ruled the catwalk. The five most famous were Naomi Campbell, Cindy Crawford, Claudia Schiffer, Linda Evangelista, and Christy Turlington. In addition to walking the runway for the biggest designers, these supermodels also appeared in advertisements, movies, and even music videos. They were paid handsomely for their work. Evangelista once famously commented about their huge paychecks, saying, "We don't wake up for less than $10,000 a day."[2]

wore long skirts paired with bobby socks and saddle shoes. Young men wore blue jeans and leather jackets, a rebellious, motorcycle-gang look made popular by movies such as *The Wild One* (1953) and *Rebel Without a Cause* (1955).

1960s and 1970s: Hippies and Counterculture

Fashion of the 1960s was an extreme reaction to the conservative styles and thinking of the 1950s. Young women ditched the long, full skirts for brightly colored, sleeveless shift dresses that got shorter and shorter. By the mid-1960s, women in London scandalized the world with miniskirts that stopped at mid-thigh. The miniskirt came to symbolize the freedom of the Swinging Sixties. Stylish hippies of the late 1960s wore stripes, psychedelic colors, and wide bell-bottom pants. Flowers and peace symbols reflected their emphasis on love and harmony. Hippie music, art, and fashions were on display at the Woodstock Music and Art Fair, held in rural Woodstock, New York in 1969.

The counterculture movement continued into the 1970s. Trendy young people embraced folk-inspired clothing that reflected global thinking. East Indian and South American fashions, such as loose, flowing caftans and ponchos, could be worn with comfortable moccasins or sandals and baggy denim bell-bottoms. For women, stiff brassieres were discarded in favor of softer bras or even a braless look.

Fashion allowed men to express themselves in ways that would have been considered too feminine in the previous decades. Glam rock stars like David Bowie wore wigs

BLUE JEANS: FROM WORKWEAR TO HIGH FASHION

The California gold rush was a chance for all types of people to strike it rich, even if they never found any gold. San Francisco businessman Levi Strauss and his partner, tailor Jacob Davis, made a fortune with their 1873 patent for riveted work pants. Made from a blue cloth called denim to hide stains, these pants were reinforced with metal rivets at seams that commonly ripped. Gold miners loved the comfortable, durable pants. Over time, these pants became known as blue jeans, or simply Levi's. By the 1960s, blue jeans had become a staple of the American closet. Today, designer blue jeans are even considered high fashion, costing more than $500 a pair.

In the 1970s, global folk styles were popular. Ringo Starr of the Beatles wears a poncho in this photo from 1970.

and makeup, while punks used tattoos, piercings, and extreme hairstyles like the Mohawk.

Even the business suits of the 1970s were a bit loud. Jackets featured wide lapels and exaggerated stitching. They were often paired with brightly colored ties or shirts.

From Power Suits to Hip-Hop Casual

The American economy soared in the 1980s. Young people were busy earning and spending money. Fashion trends reflected the new emphasis on the workforce. Women wore power suits consisting of a structured blazer and menswear-style trousers or tight skirts.

These were often made in bold colors and almost always featured dramatically padded shoulders. These outfits were called power suits for a reason—women wearing them looked imposing and powerful.

By the 1990s, women were an important part of the workforce and expected equal treatment. Women such as Princess Diana of England showed that women could be feminine in glamorous gowns and businesslike in sophisticated suits. Nicole Kidman and Gwyneth Paltrow defined Hollywood elegance in long, structured silk gowns, while hip-hop and pop artists such as Mary J. Blige and the group TLC brought baggy, urban athletic style into the limelight.

The economic boom of the 1980s redefined the way men dressed for work. Suits became sleeker, with darker colors and few dramatic details. Leisure clothes included neon exercise shorts, cut-off sweatshirts, and running shoes. They told the world a man was fit and healthy, even if he rarely wore these items to the gym! This emphasis on comfort and informal style carried

GRUNGE

In the late 1980s, flannel shirts, baggy jeans, and work boots were a stylish combination. The style, grunge, had emerged from the music scene in Seattle, Washington. Kurt Cobain, the lead singer of the band Nirvana, was a leading figure of the grunge movement. He wore his hair long and dressed in shabby, often dirty-looking clothes.

Hip-hop dancing requires baggy clothing that allows for easy movement.

into the 1990s. Men still wore suits in the workplace, but they dressed much more casually for social events. Jeans, often ripped and worn, a T-shirt, and sneakers were the standard casual outfit.

Hair and Makeup: From Bold to Natural and Back Again

Outside show business, makeup was mostly reserved for women in the second half of the twentieth century.

In the 1960s, women wore heavy black eyeliner and false eyelashes to exaggerate the eyes, a style made popular by British model Twiggy. Twiggy's mod pixie hairstyle was widely imitated, too. Men wore a version of this style called the mop top, popularized by the Beatles.

Makeup was minimal during the era of hippies and flower power of the late 1960s and 1970s, as women embraced the natural look. Both men and women wore their hair long and loose. African Americans stopped straightening their hair and wore it in a naturally curly Afro style. By the 1980s, natural was out. Hair was moussed, gelled, oiled, and set in permanent waves, or perms. Bright eye shadow, dramatic brows and lashes, and dark lips were all the rage. In the 1990s, along with the "grunge" look of ripped jeans and ratty shirts, the smoky eye became popular. Dark shadow and liner were used on the eye while the colors of the face, cheeks, and lips were muted.

Hip-Hop Style

Hip-hop, a type of music heavily influenced by rap, DJing, and MC'ing, took the 1990s by storm. Hip-hop fashion was fun and comfortable. Artists wore oversized athletic suits with a bandanna or snapback cap. Both men and women wore oversized overalls, and women often wore baggy menswear. The most iconic hip-hop shoe was the high-top basketball sneaker.

Chapter 9

Global Fashions

Fashion trends of the past emerged slowly. A king, queen, or wealthy individual would wear a certain style. The style would catch on gradually as people learned of it through word of mouth or from pictures and news stories. In modern times, television helped spread fashion more quickly. Today, trends rise and fall in an instant thanks to one invention: the Internet.

The Internet allows people all over the globe to exchange information instantaneously. The impact of the Internet on fashion is easy to see. Fashions from other parts of the world, once brought back by travelers and explorers, can be viewed online. Trends that emerge in Tokyo, Japan, quickly become popular in

The environment is a concern for fashion designers. This model at a New York Fashion Academy show wears recycled fabrics.

Kate Middleton is known for her sense of style. This blue batik-print wrap dress reportedly sold out online in minutes after Middleton wore it in 2014.

Los Angeles, California. When Kate Middleton, wife of Prince William of the United Kingdom, wears a dress to an event, customers around the world go online to purchase it. Consumers are able to see, buy, and wear new fashions in a matter of days.

Fashion in the 2000s

The first decade of the 2000s was an exciting time for fashion. Women's fashions were flirty, fun, and often very expensive. The HBO series *Sex and the City* followed the lives of four single women living in New York City, but the real star of the show was fashion. Designer shoes, handbags, and sunglasses were must-have accessories with you-must-be-kidding price tags.

One status symbol was the Hermès Birkin bag, a purse that cost more than $4,000![1] Shoes by designers Manolo Blahnik, Christian Louboutin, and Jimmy Choo were just as sought-after—and just as expensive. A single pair of Manolo Blahniks cost at least $400 at the time.[2]

Expensive designer fashions of the first part of the 2000s quickly fell out of style when the economy crashed in 2008. As in the 1970s, casual, folksy, and

THE NEW BILLIONAIRE WEAR

Historically, the world's wealthiest people were also those who dressed in the most stylish and expensive clothing. Modern billionaires, on the other hand, are opting for a much more casual style. Mark Zuckerberg, the creator of Facebook, is usually seen wearing jeans, sneakers, and a hooded sweatshirt. Microsoft founder Bill Gates usually wears casual khaki pants and a button-down shirt. These billionaires are part of a new, dressed-down generation of wealth.

bohemian clothes were all the rage. Instead of being called hippies, young people were called hipsters. They wore thrift store clothing with simple and cheap shoes, hand-me-down hats, and vintage purses.

Sustainable Fashion

Many people today are concerned about the state of the environment. Pollution, loss of natural resources, and global warming are all issues this generation will have to face. The fashion industry has historically contributed to the problem. Clothing is often made in expensive, wasteful ways. New fashion designers are hoping

Sweatshops

A sweatshop is a factory, especially a garment factory, with poor working conditions. Employees typically work long hours for very little pay, so the sweatshops can produce materials very cheaply. Many large clothing companies buy materials made in sweatshops because they are cheap. Since the Triangle Shirtwaist Fire in 1911, laws were formed to protect workers' rights, and sweatshops became less common in the United States. Today, most sweatshops are located in countries where workers have fewer rights and regulations are less strict. In 2013, a poorly-constructed building in Bangladesh that housed several garment sweatshops collapsed, killing many employees. Factories in this building made clothing for major companies, such as Walmart and Benetton. The incident raised awareness of the unfair treatment of garment industry workers and drew criticism for companies that rely on sweatshop labor.

to find better, eco-friendly ways to produce and deliver their clothes to consumers.

One way designers are helping the environment is by having their clothes made locally from locally produced fabrics. This cuts down on the fuel required to ship materials around the world. Another eco-friendly fashion trend is reusing old materials, including vintage fabrics and leathers, to make new garments.

Another way designers are helping the world is by using low-impact, sustainable, or fair trade materials. These materials are made in ways that do not hurt the environment and also benefit the people who produce them. Some clothing designers use organic fabrics. Pesticides and chemicals are not used to raise the plants or animals from which the fabrics or materials are made.

Fashion for a Cause

Today's fashion designers enjoy near-celebrity status. Michael Kors, Kate Spade, Donna Karan, and Stella McCartney are all extremely successful fashion designers who have used their fame to help charities.

One shoemaker is revolutionizing the concept of fashion for a cause. TOMS shoes, a small company located in southern California, started its "one for one" program. For every pair of shoes the company sells, TOMS gives one pair of shoes to a child in need. By 2014, the company had given away more than 10 million pairs of shoes.[3] Many other fashion companies have followed suit. Similar "buy one, give one" programs have started for school uniforms, eyeglasses, and boots.

High-Tech Style

Fashion and technology have gone hand in hand since the invention of the sewing machine. Modern fashions are no exception. Today's clothing reflects the fast-paced, high-tech, safety-conscious consumer.

One groundbreaking style invention is the Hövding, an airbag for cyclists to wear instead of a helmet. Its designers knew traditional helmets were unstylish and bulky. They created a fashionable, slim-fitting airbag that cyclists could wear around their necks.

In 2008, NASA helped Speedo design the LZR Racer swimsuit. It was lightweight and reduced friction, enabling athletes to swim incredibly fast— so fast the suit was banned from swimming competitions!

The airbag inflates and protects the head in case of collision. It comes in stylish colors and prints to match even the most chic outfit.

One of the most important accessories for today's fashion-conscious person isn't an article of clothing; it's a smartphone. These high-tech devices are helpful, entertaining, and seemingly always in use. Some fashion designers have gotten creative in the never-ending battle against draining batteries. One Dutch fashion designer created a dress with sewn-in solar panels that charge the wearer's phone. A London designer streamlined this process even further by creating a pair of pants that charge a cell phone whenever it is placed in the front pocket.

RA RA OOH LA LA

Modern fashion is wild, creative, and sometimes downright odd. Musician and artist Lady Gaga is famous for her bizarre outfits. At the 2010 MTV Music Video Awards, she stunned the world by appearing in a dress made entirely out of raw meat. Lady Gaga said the dress was meant to represent an idea. She wanted to tell people, "If we don't stand up for what we believe in, if we don't fight for our rights, pretty soon we're going to have as much rights as the meat on our bones."[4]

Fashions for Equality and the Future

The fashion community has long been accused of discrimination. Glossy magazines and fashion shows have historically showcased only very thin, white,

French designer Jean Paul Gaultier, *left*, features nontraditional models in his fashion shows. Here he is shown with Austrian model Tom Neuwirth, also known as Conchita Wurst.

able-bodied women. Today, though, this is beginning to change. Models who are plus-sized, disabled, and of many different races are being hired by the top fashion designers. Transgender models, including Carmen

Carerra, Isis King, and Ines Rau, have worked for some of the industry's biggest fashion labels. The new sense of diversity in the fashion world is greatly appreciated by people everywhere.

Reflecting on fashions of the past is a great way to start thinking about the styles that will emerge in the future. Fashion and culture are always linked. The clothes people wear reflect the issues they face in their everyday lives. Just as it is impossible to predict what the future will bring for politics, religion, and art, it is also impossible to guess what fashion will be like in the future. But one thing is for sure: it will certainly be fabulous.

Modern Haute Couture

Haute couture began in Paris in the 1850s with the work of Charles Worth and later pioneering designers such as Coco Chanel and Paul Poiret. It continues to thrive today. Haute couture fashions are ensembles that are specifically produced for individual clients. They are impeccably made from luxurious fabrics and are extremely expensive and one of a kind. Modern haute couture design houses such as Christian Dior, Jean Paul Gaultier, and Givenchy create beautiful, unique styles for celebrities, royalty, and other very wealthy consumers.

TIMELINE

c. 1300s BCE
Queen Nefertiti is an icon of ancient Egyptian fashion.

800 BCE–476 CE
In ancient Greece and Rome, simple, draped styles are in fashion for hundreds of years.

— 527–565
Justinian and Theodora rule Byzantium, bringing ornately decorated clothing into fashion throughout the empire.

1347
The Black Death arrives in Europe, killing an estimated 75 to 200 million people in the next four years. Fashion reflects the chaos in society.

1509–1547
Henry VIII rules England. He and his six wives, along with his daughter and successor, Elizabeth I, become icons of Renaissance fashion.

1642–1646
The English Civil War ushers in a period of somber fashions.

1643–1715
Louis XIV, known as the Sun King, rules France in opulent style.

1793
French Queen Marie Antoinette, famous for her over-the-top fashion, is executed along with the royal court by French revolutionary forces.

1804
Napoléon Bonaparte is crowned emperor of France. He and his wife, Josephine, wear red velvet capes at the coronation.

1846
Isaac Singer introduces the first successful sewing machine.

1851
Amelia Bloomer promotes the use of pants for women. The baggy pants become known as bloomers.

1858
English fashion designer Charles Worth opens his first fashion house in Paris. He becomes known as the father of haute couture.

TIMELINE
CONTINUED

1873
Levi Strauss patents the blue jean. These durable work pants become standard casual wear by the 1960s.

— 1900s
The S-bend corset is introduced as a healthier alternative to the traditional corset. Increasingly active lifestyles drive changes in women's fashion.

1911
A devastating fire at the Triangle Shirtwaist Company in New York City claims 146 lives and leads to reforms in the garment industry.

1914–1918
World War I forces women on the home front to take over jobs normally held by men, changing the way they dress.

1939–1945
World War II brings women into the workforce once more. Durable, comfortable styles are worn at work.

1947
French designer Christian Dior debuts the "New Look" for women: a slim waist and wide skirt.

1960s
British model Lesley Hornby, nicknamed Twiggy, becomes the face of mod British fashion.

1968
Athletes at the Summer Olympics raise black-gloved hands in a power salute to protest racism.

1980s
The American economy booms, bringing power suits with padded shoulders into style for women.

2008
Speedo invents the LZR, a swimsuit designed with the help of NASA engineers. The suit is soon banned from competition.

2010
At the MTV Video Music Awards, pop artist Lady Gaga wears a dress made of raw meat.

GLOSSARY

bloomers
Full, loose trousers gathered at the ankles. Used as athletic wear for women.

bodice
The upper part of a woman's dress.

breeches
Knee-length pants worn by men.

brocade
Silk decorated with gold and silver thread.

bustle
A pillow or set of hoops used to create fullness at the back of a skirt.

chain mail
Protective armor made of interconnected metal rings.

corset
An undergarment used to shape a woman's figure. Corsets were often tightly laced to cinch in the waist.

doublet
A short, tight jacket for men, often padded at the chest and shoulders.

farthingale
Hooped framework used to create a wide, full skirt.

haute couture
Exclusive clothing produced by top designers and fashion houses.

hose
Tight stockings.

petticoat

An underskirt used to give fullness to a woman's skirt.

ready-to-wear (prêt-à-porter)

Clothing sold off the rack in distinct sizes, rather than tailored to fit.

ruff

A stiff ring of fabric encircling the neckline.

sarcophagus

An ornate coffin.

shift

A straight dress with no waistline.

silhouette

The shape or outline of the body; in fashion, the way clothing shapes the body.

stomacher

A stiff piece of fabric worn at the front of a dress to hold in the stomach.

tunic

A simple shirtlike garment that can be slipped on over the head.

waistcoat

A long vest, often worn as part of a man's suit.

ADDITIONAL RESOURCES

Selected Bibliography

Cosgrave, Bronwyn. *The Complete History of Costume & Fashion: From Ancient Egypt to the Present Day*. New York: Checkmark, 2001. Print.

Hennessy, Kathryn, ed. *Fashion: The Definitive History of Costume and Style*. New York: DK, 2012. Print.

Stevenson, N. J. *Fashion: A Visual History from Regency & Romance to Retro & Revolution*. New York: St. Martin's, 2012. Print.

Wilcox, Ruth Turner. *Mode in Costume*. Mineola, NY: Dover, 2008. Print.

Yarwood, Doreen. *Illustrated Encyclopedia of World Costume*. Mineola, NY: Dover, 2011. Print.

Further Readings

Albee, Sarah, and Tim Gunn. *Why'd They Wear That? Fashion as a Mirror of History*. Washington, DC: National Geographic, 2015. Print.

Bingham, Jane. *A History of Fashion and Costume: The Ancient World*. New York: Facts on File, 2005. Print.

Websites

To learn more about Essential Library of Cultural History, visit **booklinks.abdopublishing.com**. These links are routinely monitored and updated to provide the most current information available.

Places to Visit

Art Institute of Chicago's Fashion Resource Center
36 South Wabash Avenue
Chicago, IL 60603
312-629-6730
http://www.saic.edu/academics/librariesandspecialcollections/
fashionresourcecenter
Visitors can examine designer garments and accessories to learn
how they are made, as well as see books, magazines, and videos
related to fashion.

Costume Institute at the Metropolitan Museum of Art
1000 Fifth Avenue
New York, New York 10028-0198
http://www.metmuseum.org/visit
Special exhibits of costumes and accessories from all over the
world are arranged every year.

Fashion Institute of Design and Merchandising (FIDM)
919 South Grand Avenue
Los Angeles, CA 90015-1421
800-624-1200
http://fidm.edu/en/Visit+FIDM/The+Campuses/Los+Angeles
Tour the school campus and fashion museum or attend the annual
runway show, DEBUT, featuring students' designs.

SOURCE NOTES

Chapter 1. The Colorful History of Fashion

1. Louis Constant Wairy. *Recollections of the Private Life of Napoleon.* Vol. 1. Trans. Walter Clark. New York: The Merriam Company, 1895. 299. *Google Book Search.* Web. 15 Sept. 2014.

2. Cathy Newman. "The Joy of Shoes." *National Geographic.* National Geographic, Sept. 2008. Web. 15 Sept. 2014.

3. Sarah Lyall. "A Traditional Royal Wedding, but for the 3 Billion Witnesses." *New York Times.* New York Times, 29 Apr. 2011. Web. 15 Sept. 2014.

Chapter 2. Ancient Fashions That Amaze

1. Jennifer Viegas. "Humans First Wore Clothing 170,000 Years Ago." *Discovery News.* Discovery, 6 Jan. 2011. Web. 15 Sept. 2014.

2. "Nefertiti." *Encyclopaedia Britannica.* Encyclopaedia Britannica, 2014. Web. 15 Sept. 2014.

3. "Neues Museum: 'In the Light of Amarna': Half a Million Visitors and Counting." *Staatliche Museen zu Berlin.* Staatliche Museen zu Berlin, 27 June 2013. Web. 15 Sept. 2014.

4. Brenda Fowler. "Forgotten Riches of King Tut: His Wardrobe." *New York Times.* New York Times, 25 July 1995. Web. 15 Sept. 2014.

5. Bronwyn Cosgrave. *The Complete History of Costume & Fashion: From Ancient Egypt to the Present Day.* New York: Checkmark, 2001. Print. 47.

6. Kathryn Hennessy, ed. *Fashion: The Definitive History of Costume and Style.* New York: DK, 2012. Print. 25.

7. Bronwyn Cosgrave. *The Complete History of Costume & Fashion: From Ancient Egypt to the Present Day.* New York: Checkmark, 2001. Print. 74.

8. Remy Melina. "Why Is the Color Purple Associated with Royalty?" *Livescience.com.* Purch, 3 June 2011. Web. 15 Sept. 2014.

9. Bronwyn Cosgrave. *The Complete History of Costume & Fashion: From Ancient Egypt to the Present Day.* New York: Checkmark, 2001. Print. 89.

10. Patrick Hunt. "Late Roman Silk: Smuggling and Espionage in the 6th Century CE." *Philolog: Classical Connections, Commentary and Critique.* Stanford University, 2 Aug. 2011. Web. 15 Sept. 2014.

Chapter 3. Fashions of the Middle Ages

1. Stephanie Pappas. "Black Death Survivors and Their Descendants Went On to Live Longer." *Scientific American.* Scientific American, 8 May 2014. Web. 15 Sept. 2014.

2. Bronwyn Cosgrave. *The Complete History of Costume & Fashion: From Ancient Egypt to the Present Day.* New York: Checkmark, 2001. Print. 113.

3. Ibid. 108.

4. Ibid. 102.

5. Kathryn Hennessy, ed. *Fashion: The Definitive History of Costume and Style.* New York: DK, 2012. Print. 45.

6. Ibid. 68.

SOURCE NOTES CONTINUED

Chapter 4. The Renaissance: A Fashion Rebirth

1. Maggie Secara. "Elizabethan Sumptuary Statutes." *Elizabethan.org.* Maggie Secara, 14 July 2001. Web. 15 Sept. 2014.

Chapter 5. From Opulence to Revolution

1. Bronwyn Cosgrave. *The Complete History of Costume & Fashion: From Ancient Egypt to the Present Day.* New York: Checkmark, 2001. Print. 172.

Chapter 6. Fashions for a Brand New World

None.

Chapter 7. Beautiful Age to Wartime

1. "Triangle Shirtwaist Factory Fire." *Encyclopaedia Britannica.* Encyclopaedia Britannica, 2014. Web. 15 Sept. 2014.
2. N. J. Stevenson. *Fashion: A Visual History from Regency & Romance to Retro & Revolution.* New York: St. Martin's, 2012. Print. 88.

Chapter 8. Anything Goes

1. Kathryn Hennessy, ed. *Fashion: The Definitive History of Costume and Style.* New York: DK, 2012. Print. 354.

2. Kiri Blakeley. "The World's Top-Earning Models." *Forbes.com.* Forbes, 16 July 2007. Web. 15 Sept. 2014.

Chapter 9. Global Fashions

1. Suzanne Pratt. "Hermes Birkin: A Good Bag but Even Better Investment." *The Street.* The Street, 26 June 2014. Web. 22 Sept. 2014. html

2. "How Luxury Brands Have Raised Prices by 60% to Increase Their Appeal." *Daily Mail.co.uk.* Daily Mail, 5 Aug. 2013. Web. 22 Sept. 2014.

3. "One for One." *TOMS.com.* TOMS Shoes, n.d. Web. 25 Sept. 2014.

4. Jillian Mapes. "Lady Gaga Explains Her Meat Dress: 'It's No Disrespect.'" *Billboard.* Billboard, 13 Sept. 2010. Web. 15 Sept. 2014.

INDEX

ABOUT THE AUTHOR

Rebecca Rissman is a nonfiction author and editor. She has written more than 200 books about history, culture, science, and art. Her book *Shapes in Sports* earned a starred review from *Booklist*, and her series *Animal Spikes and Spines* received *Learning Magazine's* 2013 Teachers Choice for Children's Books. She lives in Portland, Oregon, with her husband and daughter, and enjoys hiking, yoga, and cooking.